Papalotes

SONGS OF TEXAS

M.R. GRAHAM

Table of Contents

Introduction

I have lived in Texas all my life—every part of Texas, in fact, except El Paso. I've lived beneath the twisted live oaks of San Antonio, in the middle of the chaos of Houston, between the fragrant pines of Huntsville, upon the vast emptiness of Amarillo, on the sun-baked cement of Lubbock, the dust and mesquite of San Angelo, College Station's quiet academia, and the humid, ever-blossoming Rio Grande Valley.

It's been an enlightening life. Hollywood gives a certain impression of Texas, one that rather oddly seems to be based almost entirely on the Monument Valley rock formations in Arizona and Utah, of all places. People think of Texas as a desert, full of Stetson hats and black boots, where everybody rides horseback and talks with a twang. Few know of the never-ending miles of orange groves along the Rio Grande, or the quiet Germans and their pecan trees in Fredericksburg, the 'Keep Austin Weird' movement, or the thunderstorms that boil up in minutes and vanish again just as quickly. There is so much of Texas that never sees a silver screen: its beaches and bayous, its papayas and peaches. For every tumbleweed, there's a green valley. For every cactus pad, there's a blueberry bush.

We're not all cowboys, here. This vast land is so much more.

Spring with Claws

In early spring,
Texas sleeps beneath a veil
the shade of mockingbird down –
blue-grey –
while all below,
the wildflowers flame.
The Spring here is aptly named:
it springs with windy claws outstretched,
like a great green jaguarundi,
all wild cries and sunny teeth.

at the last

i have known this place
and here i shall return

to this place i shall return
when my heart is still
and my eyes are white
and my ribs are open to the stars

i have known this place
walked beneath pecans
in the faltering sunlight
when my eyes still saw

i have touched the limestone
with baked skin

Milagros.

Knife

Remember that little human
boy who couldn't read aloud -
who couldn't hold a pen
because his slick corn oil skin
kept sliding past itself?

Boy, oh, boy.

And he was born a hundred
years too late for his cowboy
dreams. He rides herd on the
maybes and the somedays.

He sang a knife song - one
that sliced up the rigid spines
of teachers and parents alike
and parted them before him
like God-spoken seas.
Deft elision somewhere between
his teeth and tongue, lyrical, his
words in other men's mouths.

Knife song honed with lime,
polished with manteca.

Summerbreak

Sweet and apple-crisp,

the autumn evenings fall

in twilit memory.

Gone, those autumn evenings, now.

Summer heat constricts,

cloaking skin in sweat.

Still, I have memory.

Mocking Sky

The Texas winter mocks
with dust instead of snow
and bare mesquite to testify with thorns
against a shred of weakness.

The Texas winter gusts
fiercely from the south -
grit on lips, in eyes, on tongues that wonder
where the deer drink.

The Texas winter sinks
in rust and blood and peaches
beneath the horizon. Sweetly, sweetly,
she sips the clouds.

The Texas winter clothes herself in cicada song,
and all the stars applaud.

Autumn Rains

The Texas autumn, breached,
pours forth cathartic drops,
an ecstasy of tears
to cleanse her dusty eyes of the agonizing fall.

The brow of Texas boils
in cloudy greys and thunder
amid coyote calls electric
down the city-slicker's spine
dropping low.

The breath of Texas chills -
a saw-blade through the heat -
and screams the cloud stampede
across the hills.

The voice of Texas condescends
to whisper in the huisache
and whistle in the Spanish daggers
sparring with the mockingbird
to sing before she roars.

The mercy of Texas
is no relief -

this wild trickster goddess burns

then drowns.

Morning Verse

The morning makes me reckless
with the smell of coffee curling
through my veins in electric
tendrils,
and the pen betwixt my fingertips
shooting feelers through my brain,
and a single dying star
burning in the dawn-green
East.
The morning makes me restless
with the promise of the day
and the breath of open windows
and the smooth relief of
ink;
so in the morning, like a child
celebrating life
I turn my words in dances.

Indian Summer

The Texas autumn froths
in shades of taupe and cinnamon
and lemon-scented yucca blooms -
waxen belles amid the spikes,
thickets of Jumano spears.

The Texas autumn ravages
the sunscorched clay with burning winds
that chew the live oaks all to shreds
and turn mesquites to kindling.
Wildfire breath.

The Texas autumn ticks along
in desiccated deer
yearning for a sip of winter
to ease their cracking riverbeds.

The Texas autumn flows
in rivers of molten tar
along the curbs, beneath the cars,
inexorable.

The Texas autumn breathes hard
like a woman in labor

and clings to the sun
with gifts of fiery fiddle strings
and a prayer for rain.

chaotic sky

Her hills rise and fall with her troubled breath -

this wild land of mine -

And in the turbulence of blue and gray,

her chaotic sky

twists

tangles

becomes.

Aquifer

I am far away
but the sky is very near
and the earth smells of life and limestone
My feet caked with white dust
  and oak pollen
stretch deep to find water.

Night, loving

The fire is warm,
the beer is cold,
and this is Texas

I cannot remember all the words
   to the sad coyote song
   drifting over the far ridge,
but I can sing along
   with the sandhill chorus -
   sky dark with crane wings
   and bright with stars.

Sparks soar up like
   bright ghost eyes
   of those who are not here tonight,
   stories flitting back and forth
   as we laugh
   and remember

Sweet, then

July rustles
through the leaves of the pecan,
bearing scent of limestone,
huisache blossom, and cedar,
but the surface of the river
is still,
unruffled by the whispered breath
of Texas

Holy Land

The sun-drenched hills
      are golden and gray,
      robed in cedars dark as night,
      fragrant with juniper.
In another world, this land was holy.
      This soil caked prophets' feet.
      These rivers baptized.
      These skies rained fire.
      These trees raised martyrs.
In another world, these winds spoke truths,
      and pilgrims passed in silence
      between the chalky cliffs

Pink

Prickly pears everywhere,

fuchsia stippled over green and brown,

bitter-sweet and plump, they fall

- sput! –

in a puff of Texas dust.

Don't touch; they're sharp.

Cracks

Rubbed raw, the aching soil
breaks beneath the weight
of the distant sky.

Riverbank Children

To the boy in the green canoe:

You brought a hopeful fishing pole
down here to the iron river
and with eager hands cast out your line
to plumb the depths of a crystalline morning.
The whitewashed banks lower their brows
in concentration
hungry for your disappointment.

Boy, your sweater is too large.
It covers your hands with handknit safety
and your chin with the smell of your father's cigarettes.
Boy, your chest is too small to hold
your potential. Your eyes are Concho pearls.

Did you carry that boat on your back,
young man? Does it trail behind you always?
Do you carry it to school, canoe in one hand,
while the other grips an empty bucket
reserved for the day's catch?
You are always ready, ready for a prize.

Boy, you cannot even see me up here,

merging with my park bench
in the fog – nor would I want you to.
You are the river, and her bounty is yours.
The whitewashed banks are disappointed
by your mastery, the relish and the fickle pride in a
failure.
The morning is no less sweet without a fish.

Boy, you are the river, self-absorbed, eternal;
the banks cannot stand against you.

To the girl on the playground slide:

Your pudding thighs are full of sunshine
and you gleam through the fog.
Your bare feet leave optimism in the toes-splayed tracks,
spreading down the plastic chute.
Your fingers grip the bars, clenched teeth
gritted tight, latched fast to living.

Coal-dark eyes, you black sheep girl
with your red hair bow and your mockingbird laugh,
you own the playground.
There is a woman hiding in your infant eyes.
Wild Roma queen, the world sees you falling,
but I know you fly.

The Bay Laurel and the Bird

The human animal is, in truth, a vine.
It puts down roots and sends out shoots
and flourishes in the sun.
It clings to its brick and mortar,
extends runners to embrace the walls.
It knows the soil and the light and the taste of the air.
It has counted every rock in the yard.

"I grew up in this house. I watched my brothers
throwing baseballs in the back,
my sisters twanging on Grandmother's piano.
I smelled Mother's cooking each time
I sprawled out on the carpet.
I know every ink spot speckle of Father's pen."

The average human puts down roots
and never leaves the fortress of the familiar,
even at the end.

"Bury me between the oak and the fence,
where I can see the sunset. Tell my son,
my brother, my sister, my daughter –

tell whomever that he, that she, that they
can have the old place. Just keep it in the family."

The average human molders and feeds the ants
and the grass, and soon a vine grows
up, to cling to the brick and mortar,
extends runners to embrace the walls.

I was a bay tree in a pot. My roots were
cramped and curled up tight. They sought
deep soil, but found only white beads
of artificial fertilizer. When I reached
for the sun, my shoulders hit glass.

"Plant me here! Let me taste real rain.
I have grown inside for all my life, stunted
and crabbed like a bonsai. God, please,
let me get to know the birds."

In the first place, the air was dust and
ground *comino*. My roots scratched at
the limestone they put in my pot. I felt
shells and a rusted crucifix, and mountain
laurels dropped their burning seeds
outside my window.

"Can we stay? It's spicy here, and the water
is thick with faith. I could thrust my roots
into the missions and smile at the tourists.
Here, I could be scorched, and grow, and marry,
and die."

In the second place, the air was exhaust, with
traces of shrimp and petroleum. They gave
trees to the rich and guns to the poor, in case
of hurricanes. I heard ballet and buskers rapping
for the first time.

"Can we stay? Life is so fast, here. It smells
like reality, photographed in high contrast. Things
are so tall here, so tall and black like the forests
in my dreams. Here, I could be cut, shot, and so
living is all the sweeter while it lasts."

In the third place, pines ruled the sky.
Marionberries crept up my legs and begged me
to stay,
and I wanted to,
even though it was a place where all Catholics
go to hell. I reached out, there, and felt others
reaching for me. Then they clipped my roots again
and we flew North.

"No! Let me stay, let me grow, let me live.
Let me twine my branches with the native vines!
There was light and shade and deep black earth!
There was water and birdsong and love."

In the fourth place, the sky overwhelmed. There
was wind and dust, and I was parched. The sun
blinded, and the winter cracked; my finger-leaves
bled. But there were smiles and careful hands
and a mentor, whom I miss.

"I love you, but the air has sucked me dry,
there are tumbleweeds in my hair, and the heavens
are so close, they stab my eyes. I love you, but
there is dust in my teeth. Goodbye."

In the fifth place, I flowered amid books and
other potted plants, a greenhouse. I was trimmed
and pruned and shaped. They clipped me into
a bird
changed my leaves for feathers
tore out my roots
taught my blood to run red.
I shall never land
            again.

Storm

Rain on the horizon

The brindled Texas sky

Predator-striped

Stalks

Charges

The unsuspecting land below.

Grasshoppers

Delve deep,

below the earth's flimsy crust.

Pulse without ceasing,

up and down and up,

and drink deep that Texas tea.

deluge

One palm

waves in the distance,

and the mockingbird above me

is silent,

waiting

for the deluge to begin.

Dark sky.

Dark earth.

And silence.

Lowering

Bruised sky, lowering,

dips to touch the parched soil,

and with a gentle breath,

bears far and wide

the scent

of damp earth.

It is the smell of life.

Becoming

Becoming light,

in truth I am falling,

slow and soft like motes of dust.

Downward still,

sometimes I think I am rain,

and I know the earth lies somewhere below.

Delight

The flames of autumn sear the sullen sky
with ruby, rose, carnelian, and wine,
the heady draught which slips to sparkling night,
when may the gauds of ghosts and grims combine.

mistletoe

Live oaks disdain to wither
in the dark months of shortened days.
The bare mesquite
sleeps soundly through December.
Yet in the thorny crown high above
shines mistletoe, ghostly white,
where the cardinal waits for dawn.

Wander

Winter wanderers wend their way
beneath the barren branches of huisache.
The sky is still and brilliant white,
burnished bright
by summer's vanished winds.

A New Year

I seek signs in the tangled branches

of the live oak,

silhouetted against a sickle moon.

The owl calls mysteries

which I cannot decipher,

oracles of things no pen can write.

Water whispers beyond the circle of my fire's light.

It speaks of dust and deer's hooves and living blood.

Wind, now, in the branches,

bears the distant lightning ever nearer.

Birdlife

White wings, gray wings, black wings, brown
An endless sky-rustle, brush-snap

Dove wail
Raven croak
Turkey warble

Scarlet darts beneath the leaf — pip! pip!
The cardinal has arrived.

A Sunset

The western sky melts in gold, the Texas crucible,

while pink and cream and gray climb in the east.

Indigo below, dark as the damp earth.

One star above,

the punctuation at the end of the day.

Gray

The water rushing through the channel is like steel
beyond the salt-stained granite of the jetties.
Through the mist, lights flicker, will-o-the-wisp sparkle,
luring me to the sea.
Spring Break is always like this, a burst of winter in the
Texas heat.
But somehow, I feel, the revelers on the Island do not
notice.

Black

In the night, the cicada symphony rises
shrill and eerie beneath a cloudless sky.
It is a fierce sound, that full-throated wail,
rising to a golden moon.
The road gleams wet into the distance,
trees racing past in silhouette,
black on black, a lace border to the silk heavens.
I am all goosebumps.

About M.R. Graham

M.R. Graham is a native Texan who traces strong cultural roots back to Scotland, Poland, England, and Germany. A mild-mannered university lecturer during the day, Graham transforms at night into a raging Holmesian loremaster and rabid novelist.

Though passionate about all scholarship and academia, Graham's training and true love lies with anthropology, particularly the archaeological branch.

Her writing explores the uncanny, the mystical, the mysterious, and the monstrous, seeking to capture the beauty of strangeness.

Also, steampunk and vampires.

Visit M.R. Graham at quiestinliteris.com or facebook.com/authormrgraham.

Special thanks to my dear Patrons, especially
Mr. Jim Bennett.
You can support my writing and receive early access and
special extras by contributing on Patreon at
patreon.com/mrgraham.